A Gift for

Micah Doyat

Lovingly Presented by

6/2/14

Date

Mimi's Bracelet

Salvation Crystal Clear for Children

Copyright © 2013 by Legacy Literature Classics, LLC.

Library of Congress Cataloging-in-Publication Data:
Camperson, Sherry Hutson,
Mimi's bracelet: salvation crystal clear for children;
illustrated by Jana Camperson.

ISBN 978-0-9913627-0-7

All photographs by Jana Camperson, except those
individually credited.

Digital art (front and back covers) by Cheri MacCallum,
www.artbycheri.com.

Original oil painting (back cover) by Eugenia Tucker.

"Happy Spiritual Birthday" lyrics by Sherry Camperson.

Mimi's Bracelet can be purchased in quantity for church,
ministry, missions, educational, business, fund-raising,
and promotional purposes. Please contact Sherry Hutson
Camperson by email at shcamperson@aol.com, or online at legacyliteratureclassics.com or mimisbracelet.com.

All Scripture references are from the King James Bible.

Printed in the USA.

Also by Sherry Hutson Camperson

Order in the Court
(How You Can Enjoy an Orderly Life)

Go for the Gold
(A Life of Excellence)

Sailing Away
(Video Biography of Curtis Hutson)

O, Beautiful Star of Bethlehem
(Christmas Video with the Curtis Hutson Family)
(Instrumental Christmas CD)

Old-Time Preacher Man
(Curtis Hutson Music CD)

On the Winning Side
(Alan Camperson Music CD)

Kids Grow Up
(Alan Camperson Music CD for Children)

The Hutson Sisters
Trio Music CDs

To learn more about
Legacy Literature Classics
Contact:

Sherry Hutson Camperson
P.O. Box 215
Buford, GA 30515
shcamperson@aol.com
www.legacyliteratureclassics.com
www.mimisbracelet.com

Dedicated to our precious grandsons,
Jake and Graham,

and to all the other children God sends
into our lives to love and to lead.

"Nothing of much significance happens to a child after age twelve."

Sir James M. Barrie (1860-1937), Author
The Boy Who Wouldn't Grow Up
Performed today as Peter Pan

"I believe if one guardian angel descended to earth and found one poor, ragged boy or girl, without father or mother, he would wing his way back to Heaven. There he would talk to God about that needy child who had no one to care for him and teach him the way of life. If God were to ask among the throng of angels who was willing to come down to this earth and live here for fifty years and lead that one to Jesus Christ, every angel would volun- teer to come. Even Gabriel who stands in the presence of the Almighty would say, 'Let me leave my high and lofty position, and let me have the luxury of leading one soul to Jesus Christ.' There is no greater honor than to be the instrument in God's Hands of leading one person out of the kingdom of Satan into the glorious light of Heaven." D. L. Moody

"If I could relive my life, I would devote my entire ministry to reaching children for God."

Dwight L. Moody

"But Jesus said, Suffer [let or allow] little children, and forbid them not, to come unto me: for of such is the kingdom of heaven" (Matthew 19:14). In many cases, adults must be compelled toward the Saviour. Luke 14:23 tells us so. "And the lord said unto the servant, Go out into the highways and hedges, and compel them to come in, that my house may be filled." But Matthew 18:3 says, "Verily I say unto you, Except ye be converted, and become as little children, ye shall not enter into the kingdom of heaven." Because Jesus said each of us must come to Him like a child, we ought never doubt that our little ones can understand and come to the Saviour early in life.

I am grateful to God for my family and friends who have inspired and supported this evangelistic effort. I thank God for leading me to the finest of consecrated talents—photographers, artists, editors, designers, jewelers, attorneys, businessmen and businesswomen, pastors, evangelists, and prayer partners—who share my burden for the souls of men, women and children. They have graciously contributed their talents and time. And I have trusted the clear guidance of the Blessed Holy Ghost every step—and every stop—along the way.

Please pray with all of us that many young people will receive this unique gift book and accept God's beautiful gift of salvation as told through the eyes of a child—our first grandson, Jake.

May God bless you always . . . and in all ways,

Sherry Camperson

Sherry Hutson Camperson

Taking Penny's sacrosanct request seriously, I sedulously sought the Lord's guidance for the best way to accomplish this worthy work. Through much prayer and study, I was inspired to follow the path prepared by those who have come before me.

On January 11, 1866, Charles Haddon Spurgeon preached to orphaned children in London, England. His text was Psalm 51:7, "Wash me, and I shall be whiter than snow." Yearning to reach both head and heart, Spurgeon used the visual aid of a book of colors—black, red, and white. The young reader of this book without words learned of salvation in an elementary fashion.

Black represented the sinful state in which each of us was born. Red represented the blood of Jesus Christ, which He willingly shed on the Cross for our sins. White represented the pureness we are given by God through the cleansing sacrifice of His Son, Jesus Christ.

By 1875, both Charles H. Spurgeon and Dwight L. Moody were using a booklet with a fourth color, gold, representing the streets of pure gold in Heaven. In 1939, Child Evangelism Fellowship added the color green to represent spiritual growth.

The colors are simply tools to help children remember the message. The meaning of each color is supported with Scriptures. The colors have been creatively displayed on soccer balls, banners, scarves, beads, ropes, and in many other ways. In our true story, the only way to Heaven is taught through a colorful crystal charm bracelet—Mimi's bracelet.

Mother, father, grandmother, grandfather, and teacher—take interest every time your precious little person inquires about salvation. Answer his questions no matter if you see "lights coming on" or not. Piling God's Word upon little heads and hearts is not a waste of your time. Like the snow of winter melts when the sun returns, the information you prayerfully deliver to the minds of your little loved ones will lie in waiting until the Holy Ghost's warm illumination distills the Word directly into their hearts.

The Story Behind Our Story

D. L. Moody once said that at a church gathering two and a half people were converted to Christ. A friend asked if he meant two adults and a child. No, instead Moody was speaking of two children and one adult. You see, when a child is led to Christ, a whole life is saved!

My precious father, Curtis W. Hutson (1934-1995), was a preacher and publisher of God's good tidings of salvation. His books, booklets, and tracts have been distributed around the world by the millions. Always making the plan of salvation clear, he was an instrument God used to bring tens of thousands to the cleansing blood of Jesus Christ—I being one of them at age eight.

Like D. L. Moody before him, Curtis Hutson knew the importance of reaching children for Christ. He commissioned me to write for children, and under his editorship I supplied a column titled "Children's Challenge." Daddy asked me to continue writing for the children.

At a ladies' conference in California, a dear pastor's wife came to me expressing a need. Penny had searched for a book to pass along to children—one easy enough for a young child to read and understand God's simple plan of salvation. She never found such a book. Because she knew my father had written a best-selling and award-winning book on the subject of salvation, the Lord put it on her heart to ask me to tell the old, old story, crystal clear, for children.

"Rev. Jesse Irvin Overholtzer, founder of Child Evangelism Fellowship in 1937, grew up in a religious family. At age twelve, he was convicted of his own sin and sought counsel from his mother who said, 'Son, you are too young.' It wasn't until Overholtzer was in college that he heard the Gospel and trusted Christ as his Saviour. Later as a pastor, Mr. Overholtzer read Charles Spurgeon's sermons which stated, 'A child properly instructed, can believe as truly and be regenerated as an adult.'

"At every step in leading a child to Christ, pray for, look for, and expect the Holy Ghost to convict of sin, to reveal the truth of the Gospel, and to illumine the child's mind so he can grasp the saving truth."

Jesse Irvin Overholtzer, CEF

The Lord used this statement to lead Mr. O, as he was affectionately called, to begin the ministry of Child Evangelism Fellowship at age sixty. His desire was to tell boys and girls how to be free from the guilt of sin, something which no one would tell him when he was a boy." (The Indomitable Mr. O by Norman Rohrer)

Papa gave Mimi a bracelet for her birthday. I asked Mimi how old she was. "Why, Jake," she said, "I'm old enough to be your grandmother!" Everyone laughed. You see, Mimi is my grandmother!

Mimi's bracelet is so pretty . . .

. . . with sparkling crystal stones and shiny silver charms. It is a beautiful bracelet! Papa loves Mimi very much.

But I have trusted in thy mercy; my heart shall rejoice in thy salvation. –Psalm 13:5

Rejoice, because your names are written in heaven. –Luke 10:20

By the way, my name is Jake. I want to tell you the best true story I have ever heard. Will you let me tell you what puts this happy smile on my face and keeps joy in my heart?

These things have I written unto you that believe on the name of the Son of God; that ye may know that ye have eternal life. –1 John 5:13

Verily, verily, I say unto you, He that believeth on me hath everlasting life. –John 6:47

This is Mimi's new bracelet. Mimi used her bracelet to show me how I could live forever. Would you like to know how to live forever? Please let me tell you the crystal-clear story Mimi told me from her new bracelet.

Let's look at the Bible—the very first silver charm on Mimi's bracelet. The Bible is God's letter to us and tells us how He made us and loves us. The Bible tells us God is always good and honest and kind. God knows everything. The Bible is not everything God knows. The Bible tells us everything God wants us to know about how to live forever in Heaven with Him.

Every word of God is pure: he is a shield unto them that put their trust in him. –Proverbs 30:5

And that from a child thou hast known the holy scriptures, which are able to make thee wise unto salvation through faith which is in Christ Jesus. –II Timothy 3:15

For the prophecy came not in old time by the will of man: but holy men of God spake as they were moved by the Holy Ghost. –II Peter 1:21

We love him, because he first loved us. –I John 4:19

So then faith cometh by hearing, and hearing by the word of God. –Romans 10:17

God is everywhere, and He made everything—the earth, the waters, and the sky. God created you and me, too. He is building a happy home for us in Heaven where no one says mean words or does bad things. In Heaven, there is no sadness and no tears. No one hurts or gets sick or dies there. Heaven is a perfect place and very beautiful, too. The gold crystal makes us think about the golden streets in Heaven. I really want to go there and live forever, don't you?

All things were made by him; and without him
was not any thing made that was made. –John 1:3

God that made the world and all things therein,
seeing that he is Lord of heaven and earth. –Acts 17:24

So God created man in his own image, in the image of God
created he him; male and female created he them. –Genesis 1:27

And God shall wipe away all tears from their eyes; and there shall be no
more death, neither sorrow, nor crying, neither shall there be any more
pain: for the former things are passed away. -Revelation 21:4

In my Father's house are many mansions:
if it were not so, I would have told you. I go to
prepare a place for you. –John 14:2

For he hath made him to be sin for us, who knew no sin; that we might be made the righteousness of God in him.
–II Corinthians 5:21

Righteous Judge
Saviour
I AM
Only Wise God
Our Dwelling Place
Mighty One
Everlasting God
Creator
LORD Almighty
El Shaddai
Redeemer
KING OF GLORY
GOD THE FATHER
MY ROCK
Most High

For God so loved the world, that he gave his only begotten Son, that whosoever believeth in him should not perish, but have everlasting life.
–John 3:16

For the wages of sin is death; but the gift of God is eternal life through Jesus Christ our Lord.   –Romans 6:23

Look at His Cross. God shows us how much He loves us. God made a wonderful plan, but it was not easy for Him. God sent His only Son, Jesus Christ, to suffer and die on the Cross. Jesus never did anything wrong, so He did not deserve to suffer. But He agreed to be punished for all our sins—yours and mine. Jesus paid for our sin on the Cross of Calvary so we could go to Heaven and live with Him forever. God gave us the gift of His Only Son, Jesus.

The dark stone reminds us of sin. Sin is anything we do that does not please God. Telling lies or taking things that do not belong to us is sin. Disobeying our parents is sin. We all have sinned. Sin hurts the people God loves. He hates sin and will not let sin into Heaven. God made an awful place where sin will be punished forever. That place is Hell, but it was not made for you! Your sin makes God very sad. He loves you and wants you to live with Him in Heaven forever. Because God is loving, good, honest and kind, He did something very special for you and me so we can be forgiven.

[The] everlasting fire [was] prepared for the devil and his angels. —Matthew 25:41

Wherefore, as by one man [Adam] sin entered into the world, and death by sin; and so death passed upon all men, for that all have sinned. —Romans 5:12

For all have sinned, and come short of the glory of God. — Romans 3:23

The heart is deceitful above all things, and desperately wicked: who can know it? –Jeremiah 17:9

There is none that doeth good, no, not one. –Romans 3:12

But there is a problem with my heart. My heart could keep me from going to Heaven. We were all born with something bad in our hearts that can never be allowed in Heaven. That is sin. Sin in our hearts makes us want to do wrong things.

Judge

viour

Redeemer

El Shaddai

LORD Almighty

God

Christ died for our sins according to the scriptures; And that he was buried, and that he rose again the third day according to the scriptures.   –I Corinthians 15:3-4

Without shedding of blood is no remission [forgiveness of sin].   –Hebrews 9:22

The red crystal reminds us of His blood. Because He loved us, Jesus, the perfect Son of God, gave His precious blood. He died, He was buried, and He rose from the grave for you and for me. Now we don't have to be punished for our sin. Instead, Jesus was punished for us. Our sins can be forgiven. Now Jesus can save us from the punishment of sin. The Bible tells us so.

See the praying hands at the center of Mimi's bracelet. Prayer is how we talk to God. Do you agree with God about your sin? Tell Him. Will you admit that you have done wrong? Tell Him so. Do you believe Jesus died on the Cross for your sins and rose from the grave? Thank Him. Do you want Jesus to forgive your sins? Ask Him. Do you believe Jesus is God and the only way to Heaven? Believe Him. Will you trust Him to take you to Heaven? You can trust Him. Will you pray and receive the Lord Jesus Christ as your Saviour? Pray and receive Him now.

For by grace are ye saved through faith; and that not of yourselves: it is the gift of God: Not of works, lest any man should boast.
-Ephesians 2:8-9

He that believeth on him is not condemned: but he that believeth not is condemned already, because he hath not believed in the name of the only begotten Son of God. -John 3:18

Jesus saith unto him, I am the way, the truth, and the life: no man cometh unto the Father, but by me.
-John 14:6

If thou shalt confess with thy mouth the Lord Jesus, and shalt believe in thine heart that God hath raised him from the dead, thou shalt be saved.-Romans 10:9

Believe on the Lord Jesus Christ, and thou shalt be saved.
-Acts 16:31

I acknowledged my sin unto thee, and mine iniquity have I not hid. I said, I will confess my transgressions unto the Lord; and thou forgavest the iniquity of my sin. -Psalm 32:5

Repent ye therefore, and be converted, that your sins may be blotted out.   -Acts 3:19

While we were yet sinners, Christ died for us.-Romans 5:8

He that believeth on the Son hath everlasting life: and he that believeth not the Son shall not see life; but the wrath of God abideth on him.
-John 3:36

Behold, now is the accepted time; behold, now is the day of salvation.   -II Corinthians 6:2

Dear Lord Jesus, I know I am a sinner, and I deserve to pay for my own sin. I do believe that You died to pay what I owe for my sin. Today, the best I know how, I trust You as my Saviour. I will depend on You from this moment on for my salvation. Thank You for loving me and for saving me. Now help me to live for You and be a good Christian. Amen.

For whosoever shall call upon the name of the Lord shall be saved.   –Romans 10:13

Believe on the Lord Jesus Christ, and thou shalt be saved.   –Acts 16:31

Verily, verily, I say unto you, He that heareth my word, and believeth on him that sent me, hath everlasting life, and shall not come into condemnation; but is passed from death unto life.   –John 5:24

Point to the clear crystal. Now our hearts are clean. The blood of Jesus Christ has washed our hearts that were dirty with sin. Salvation is crystal clear to me. I understand. Do you understand? I am God's child by faith in Jesus Christ. Do you believe Jesus? Then you are a child of God, too. We are going to Heaven because of what Jesus did for us. Thank you Jesus!

Now ye are clean through the word
which I have spoken unto you.
–John 15:3

God is light, and in him is no darkness at all.
–I John 1:5

Wash me, and I shall be whiter than snow.
–Psalm 51:7

But as many as received him, to them gave
he power to become the sons of God,
even to them that believe on his name.
–John 1:12

For ye are all the children of
God by faith in Christ Jesus.
–Galatians 3:26

Look at the music notes. When we become God's child, we want
to sing about Him and praise His Wonderful Name. He likes to
hear our voices tell of His goodness and greatness. I love to
sing. I love to sing about Jesus!

O sing unto the Lord a
new song; for he hath
done marvellous things.
–Psalm 98:1

O come, let us sing unto the
Lord: let us make a joyful noise
to the rock of our salvation.
–Psalm 95:1

And he hath put a new song
in my mouth, even praise unto
our God.
–Psalm 40:3

Speaking to yourselves in psalms and hymns
and spiritual songs, singing and making melody
in your heart to the Lord.
–Ephesians 5:19

Let the word of Christ dwell in you richly in all
wisdom; teaching and admonishing one another
in psalms and hymns and spiritual songs,
singing with grace in your hearts to the Lord.
–Colossians 3:16

O Lord, open thou my lips; and my mouth
shall shew forth thy praise.
–Psalm 51:15

Be ye therefore
followers of God,
as dear children.
-Ephesians 5:1

Those that be planted in
the house of the LORD, shall
flourish in the courts of our God.
-Psalm 92:13

But grow in grace, and in the knowledge
of our Lord and Saviour Jesus Christ. To
him be glory both now and for ever. Amen.
-II Peter 3:18

Gaze at the green crystal. Green reminds of us of growing
things, like trees and grass. Plants and flowers need water
and sunshine to grow. God wants us to grow as His children.
We grow closer to Jesus by reading and hearing His Word,
the Holy Bible. We grow by spending time with others who
love Him, too. We grow by talking to Jesus every day when
we pray. Jesus wants us to follow His example and become
more like Him. He will help us do what is right.

Someone cried, "Where must this seed be sown
To bring the most fruit when it is grown?"
The Master heard, then said as He smiled,
"Go plant it for Me in the heart of a child!"
-Anonymous

See the shiny, silver key? Every promise in the Bible is a key to your happiness and joy. Now that you have asked Jesus to forgive you and to be your Saviour, all of His promises are for you—God's child. Jesus promises to never leave us. That is one of my favorite Bible promises.

For he hath said, I will never leave thee, nor forsake thee.
–Hebrews 13:5

And being fully persuaded that, what he had promised, he was able also to perform. –Romans 4:21

And this is the promise that he hath promised us, even eternal life. –I John 2:25

Let us hold fast the profession of our faith without wavering; (for he is faithful that promised).– Hebrews 10:23

Whereby are given unto us exceeding great and precious promises. –II Peter 1:4

The blue crystal reminds us of the sky that covers the world. Like the sky, the Holy Ghost is everywhere and is always with us. He sees all we do, hears everything we say, and always knows how we feel. We need Him. His name means helper. He will help us pray. He will help us understand the Bible. He will warn us of sin and help us do good. You can always trust the Holy Ghost to lead you in the right way. Listen to His still, small voice. Obey Him. Follow Him.

[The LORD speaks in] a still small voice. -I Kings 19:12

But the Comforter, which is the Holy Ghost, whom the Father will send in my name, he shall teach you all things, and bring all things to your remembrance, whatsoever I have said unto you. -John 14:26

For as many as are led by the Spirit of God, they are the sons of God. -Romans 8:14

And when he is come, he will reprove the world of sin. -John 16:8

There is a tiny mirror on Mimi's bracelet. It is the last charm. Why do we use a mirror? We want to see what we look like. If our faces are dirty, we can wash them. If our hair is messed up, we can comb it. If our clothes are not clean, we can change them. Mimi says she uses two mirrors when she gets ready in the morning! Why does she need two mirrors?

For if any be a hearer of the word, and not a doer, he is like unto a man beholding his natural face in a glass. —James 1:23

Yes, Mimi needs two mirrors—one for the outside and another for the inside! One mirror is her looking glass. But the Word of God—the Holy Bible—is the mirror for her heart. It is important how we look on the outside, but it is more important how we look on the inside. The glass mirror shows us the outside. But the mirror of His Word tells us what is right or wrong on the inside. So we are back to the beginning of Mimi's bracelet—the Bible—where our story started.

Draw nigh to God, and he will draw nigh to you. Cleanse your hands, ye sinners; and purify your hearts.
–James 4:8

For ye are bought with a price: therefore glorify God in your body, and in your spirit, which are God's.
–I Corinthians 6:20

I love birthdays! I'm glad everybody has one. I like cake and ice cream, too. It is fun to make a wish and blow out all the candles. I really like presents. It is fun to celebrate life and being born.

Marvel not that I said unto thee, Ye must be born again.   –John 3:7

I am so glad Mimi had a birthday. I am thankful for her beautiful bracelet that showed me how I can have two birthdays every year. I have been born again! I always celebrate my first birth, when I was born into my family. And now I will celebrate my second birth, when I was born into God's Family.

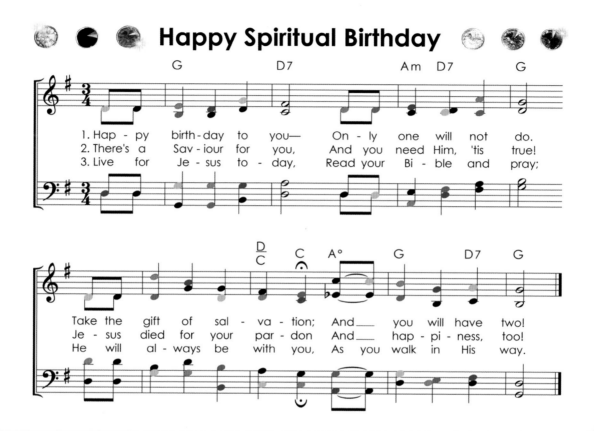

The sacred origin of the original Happy Birthday song is befitting to our use of it here with the new lyrics provided by Sherry Camperson (Mimi). In 1893, two Sunday school teachers from Kentucky composed the simple original lyrics and popular melody of this beloved song. Patty S. Hill, an influential elementary school teacher and principal, and her sister, Mildred J. Hill, an accomplished concert pianist and composer, wrote it as a greeting song with which to welcome their students to class. Never married and without children, these Southern belles continue to touch the lives of children—of all ages—as their lasting legacy is sung at most every birthday celebration around the world. Celebrate your spiritual birthday with the singing of this song we have included for you.

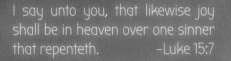

I say unto you, that likewise joy
shall be in heaven over one sinner
that repenteth.   –Luke 15:7

Every time someone believes on Jesus Christ and receives His gift of salvation, there is a spiritual birthday party in Heaven. The people in Heaven celebrate when we are born again.

Remember what you have learned from each color. See how all the colors have come together to tell us the best true story we have ever heard. I am so excited about God's gift of salvation. I could not wait to tell my brother, Graham. And now I have told you! Let's thank God for all He has done for us. When you hear good news, you just want to share it, right? Now go tell someone about Mimi's bracelet and what you have learned about salvation—crystal clear!

When He Cometh

by William O. Cushing

When He cometh, when He cometh
To make up His jewels,
All His jewels, precious jewels,
His loved and His own.

Like the stars of the morning,
His brightness adorning,
They shall shine in their beauty,
Bright gems for His crown.

He will gather, He will gather
The gems for His kingdom;
All the pure ones, all the bright ones,
His loved and His own.

Little children, little children,
Who love their Redeemer,
Are the jewels, precious jewels,
His loved and His own.

Spiritual Birth Certificate

_____

(Date)

_____

(Your Name)

_____

(Place)

Your Testimony in Your Own Words

_____

_____

_____

_____

Since you have believed on the Lord Jesus Christ and have trusted Him to take you to Heaven, let us know so we can rejoice with you. We will pray for you to grow and learn more about living for Jesus and telling others about Him.

Contact us by email or online at
shcamperson@aol.com
www.legacyliteratureclassics.com
www.mimisbracelet.com

Mail correspondence to
Mimi and Jake Camperson
P. O. Box 215
Buford, Georgia 30515

The Danger of Delay
by Curtis W. Hutson

On October 5, 1975, my father-pastor, Curtis W. Hutson, presented a salvation sermon to his thriving congregation, as was his custom most every Sunday morning for the twenty-one years he was their pastor. As an example pastor, he led the church to record-breaking state and national attendance and membership numbers. But his real reason for living was to exhaust his every breath by telling folks how to know Jesus Christ as their own personal Saviour. The following is a portion of that sobering sermon, "The Danger of Delay." Its truths remain ever relevant today.   –SHC

Each week, our bus director, John Stancil, and I are thrilled to watch the children bound off the church buses and file into their Sunday school classes. I'm thrilled to see them accept Christ when they are young and their hearts are open to the Gospel. "But Jesus said, Suffer [let or allow] little children, and forbid them not, to come unto me: for of such is the kingdom of heaven" (Matthew 19:14). Children easily accept God's gift of salvation if we will only allow them to come and do not stand in their way.

A survey of one thousand Christians was conducted, and it was discovered that out of one thousand, a total of seven hundred seventy-six (776) accepted Christ before age twelve. Think of that! The truth of the matter is that the majority of folks are saved as children. (I was saved when I was eleven years old.) Seventy-five percent of those surveyed were saved before age twelve. That means if you are over twelve years old, your chances of being saved (on the average) are only twenty-five percent. Of course, God still loves you and will accept you, but your chances are frightening.

If you're over fifteen years old, your chances have been reduced to ten percent. If you're over twenty-five years old, your chances of ever accepting Christ are a mere five percent. And if you're over thirty-five years old, your chances are down to only one percent—only one out of every hundred. Age diminishes the likeliness you'll ever make the decision to follow Christ. There is danger in delay.

Older folks who have rejected Christ often bear a stern, hardened countenance. Their hearts are hardened because they've said, "No," to God so many times. True conviction now eludes them. The following is a fable, but it illustrates what I am trying to say:

> Long ago the Devil called all the demons of Hell together to devise a scheme to damn the souls of men. Suggestion after suggestion was offered. A brilliant demon said, "Let's tell men about the Bible and that it is God's Word. Let's tell men Heaven and Hell are real. And let's tell them that God loves them and made a way for everyone to go to Heaven by sending His Only Son, Jesus Christ, to take their punishment for sin. Let's go ahead and tell them that people who die without the Saviour suffer eternal fire in Hell. And let's tell men that

people who believe in Christ will enjoy the Glories of Heaven forever in the Hereafter. But let's tell them to wait—don't rush this decision. Assure men that they can trust Christ later—but not now. All the demons of Hell applauded their brilliant cohort. Satan said, "That's it! That's what we'll do. Men will delay this important decision and damn their own souls."

Of course, no meeting like that ever took place, but judging by my own experience as a pastor and soulwinner, I believe Satan's chief instrument in steering men to Hell truly is delay. Just keep putting it off. The experience that is life will harden your heart, and you will eventually die without the Saviour. What can be done anytime is never done at all!

Hell is populated with procrastinating people. Felix and Agrippa are two Bible examples. When Paul, the king's prisoner, gave his own testimony of salvation on the Damascas Road, King Agrippa responded, "Almost thou persuadest me to be a Christian" (Acts 26:28).

Then there was Felix, who "sent for Paul, and heard him concerning the faith in Christ. And as he reasoned of righteousness, temperance, and judgment to come, Felix trembled, and answered, Go thy way for this time; when I have a convenient season, I will call for thee" (Acts 24:24-25). The Bible never records Felix calling for Paul again. If Felix did not find a convenient time, then he died and lifted his eyes in Hell. He's there, not because he wanted to go, but because he waited too late.

It is ironic that Satan tells people to wait until they feel more like it. The Devil discouraged me hundreds of times before I trusted Christ. He would say, "Wait until you feel more like it." Using deception, he knew all the time that I felt more like believing God then than I would ever feel in the future.

The truth of the matter is every time you reject Jesus Christ your heart becomes harder and harder. After awhile, God speaks, and you don't even hear His Voice. The Devil knows you will lose your desire to respond to Christ. You lose sensitivity to God's Holy Ghost. There is danger in delay.

If you've never trusted Christ as your Saviour, receive Him as your Saviour now! You can be saved today and know you are on your way to Heaven. Please don't wait another second!

If God speaks to your heart in any measure at all, if He tugs just a little bit, thank God you can still detect Him. Accept God's beautiful plan of salvation—put it off no longer. Procrastination is precarious. Delay is dangerous.

Mimi's Bracelet™ is fashionably worn, opening opportunities to charmingly share the sweet salvation story. Mimi's Bracelet™ is an attractive gift for Christmas, Easter, Mother's Day, birthdays, anniversaries and other special occasions.

If you would like to give this special bracelet to your mother, grandmother, aunt, teacher or yourself, contact Mimi for its availability.

Sherry Hutson Camperson
P. O. Box 215
Buford, Georgia 30515

shcamperson@aol.com
www.legacyliteratureclassics.com
www.mimisbracelet.com

About the Author
Sherry Hutson Camperson

Smith Studio of Photography

Sherry was born in Atlanta, Georgia and raised as a PK (Preacher's Kid). The firstborn daughter of Dr. and Mrs. Curtis Hutson, she, along with her two sisters and only brother, was "drugged" as a child. Yes, she was "drug" to church, "drug" to Sunday school, and "drug" to revival meetings. Some critics expected the Hutson children would weary of church and forsake the House of God when they grew up. But to the Glory of God and the joy of their parents, all the daughters married preachers, and Sherry's only brother is a preacher, too.

Dr. and Mrs. Rick Camperson, Sr.

Sherry became a PW (Preacher's Wife) when she married Rick Camperson, who has pastored in the Greater Atlanta area for thirty years. God has blessed Rick and Sherry with three wonderful children.

Jana, their youngest child and only daughter, is a photographer. Curt is a golf professional and musician. Alan, their firstborn son, is married to Anna; and they enjoy their lives together in the ministry of music. Alan and Anna have given Rick and Sherry two grandsons: Jake, who is six, and Graham, who is three.

When Alan was ordained into the Gospel ministry, another credential was added behind Sherry's name—PM (Preacher's Mother). I guess one could say Sherry's life has come full circle with an extent of experience that helps her understand the unique needs of the pastor's home from three perspectives—PK, PW, and PM. It is truly a life worth living! To God be the Glory.

Sherry has produced two video biographies of her father's life and ministry, <u>Sailing Away</u> and <u>O, Beautiful Star</u>. She is the author of <u>Order in the Court</u> and <u>Go for the Gold</u> and has produced nine music CDs (of her father, of her son, and with her sisters). Along with writing, Sherry enjoys singing, teaching and speaking at ladies' conferences and interpreting for the deaf community. You will notice she is subtly signing "I love you" to her husband who was present while she posed for the portrait used on the back cover. Of her various responsibilities, Sherry most enjoys being a wife, mother, and grandmother.

Today Sherry is serving the Lord in any way He wants to use her and influencing their children and grandchildren for the service of the King. "Those that be planted in the house of the Lord shall flourish in the courts of our God" (Psalm 92:13). Her love for children, along with an Elementary Education degree and twenty-five years of home-schooling, has excited, equipped and experienced Sherry to fashion the book you hold in your hand.